MONDAY MATTERS 1

START YOUR WEEK
WITH INSPIRATION AND
INSIGHT!

CAROLINE BEARDALL

MONDAY
MATTERS 1

CONTENTS

INTRODUCTION

Being a successful business – private or public sector – means actually caring about your people not just saying you do. Being a successful human is doing the right thing even when no one is looking. My favourite idiom is 'the standard you walk past is the standard you accept' and whether that's in the office, the home, the supermarket, on the bus, in a queue, travelling or simply getting up in the morning and going to work, I think Monday matters to set the week up well, and I thought you might think so to – or give it to someone who needs to know!

In March 2023 I decided to start every working week with a positive business focussed intention, to work well and achieve my purpose of shining through others, to help make the difference for others to succeed. I started posting on Linked In. People read my posts (thousands of them! Every week!). Then I thought 'wouldn't it be handy to have a years' worth to work through or dip into for moments that matter? And for non-LinkedIn-ers! So, I wrote a years' worth. And here it is.

Every one of the stories in Monday Matters is true, they are real life events that happen all around us. By noticing, guiding, and illuminating these I share my thoughts with the hope that others may be inspired, have an 'ah-ha' moment or feel like someone – me – is alongside them as they find their best selves, solve their trickiest moments and issues, and know that they are simply not alone and can succeed from wherever they start.

The journey of life and experience means that you cannot know everything at the beginning – that would spoil the story anyway! – so I am sharing some insights to perhaps create a couple of short cuts and a working world which really is better for all individuals and organisations..

ALTRUISM

Why do we do things for others? What's in it for me? Or the 'bottom line'? And when we do something for someone are we actually serving ourselves somehow?

What about a small thing? Something like giving up a seat or opening a door for someone? Is it to help without anything in return, or maybe just giving what we can when we have 'extra' (be that time, energy, money or food) – would you be so generous when you haven't got time or tired feet? Or maybe you get offended when someone opens a door for you or offers a seat as you see it as patronising? Or do you simply pay it forward?

What about our colleagues, or to meet our performance targets (for ourselves, team or company), do we give just what's needed or what only we can, or do we give everything we have to help others too and go above and beyond?

I suppose it depends where you start, how your view of the world shapes the answer to that, but I reflect that those who keep a tight hold on all they have and do not offer generously are the ones who eventually squeeze the life out of others and themselves and so the possibility of an enduring addition to life's rich tapestry falls away. Takers are always takers and givers always givers but the most dangerous I have found are the takers who show up as givers – or even on some level believe they are givers! The 'reframing' of a narrative to help one be shown in a better light is also another burden to be carried. Maybe St Ignatius had it right "to give and not to count the cost". Maybe. What can you give to make Monday matter today?

BEST FRIEND

I met my best friend in the loo. I had been chairing a meeting for a national project and had a bit of 'drive' about me – those who know me will get what I mean! I haven't changed much in all those years! And in the 'let's take a comfort break for 10 minutes' after a particularly 'testing' item on the agenda I repaired to the sanctuary of a cubicle in the washroom to have some reset time!

Within seconds I heard a voice say "that Caroline is impossible, she wants it all and never gives up, what is she? The Duracell bunny?" And those you who remember that advert will know the era I refer to! But this, now friend, then a voice from the other side of the cubicle door went on. She complained about my expectations my need for focus and my duty to deliver but interestingly she 'got it' that I was so committed to the cause we were focussed on and I had such great ambition for the outcome – not for myself. She saw my steel, my style, but also my care which drove me (and her and others) perhaps a little too hard.

Never once have I been sorry to have heard what she said 'behind closed doors' about me, nor was she afraid at any point to stand by her assessment and assertion.

True it was an interesting moment when I unlocked the door and stepped into the washbasin area!! But she was right, in every count, and she was and is a fantastic colleague, friend, influencer and person who I respect and admire to this day. I have a friendship that lasts whatever the circumstances and whether I am up or down it started with honesty and care and is still that to this day, over 25 years later. Will you make a friend today in an unexpected way or speak a truth that helps the other and yourself have a bond for life. Look out for it, don't take offence, this Monday might matter more than you know!

– 3 –

BUSKING

Don't you just love that haunting sound of the jazz sax that you hear floating up to greet you while you descend the escalator into the underworld of the London tube? Aaahhhh… Doo doo dah doo, bah dee dee dee dee doo doo dah doo… Makes me think of all those seedy dark old smoke-filled bars I have never been in (?!) with riffs being played by the likes of Miles Davis, John Coltrane and Charlie Parker.

In fact, if I try really hard, I can love most of the buskers on the London Underground for their skill and being lost in the sounds, but it has become a little 'gentrified'. Booking a slot to busk? I suppose it's one up from no busking but it's not quite the spirit, eh?

I busked with my sister in York one Winter when we were young… her on the flute and me on, was it really the French horn?! Yup, 'fraid to say it was. And I fear that at that time we might have been on the end of what my dear husband sometimes says 'how much to make them stop'!? when the sound is closer to strangulation than music. But it got us cold and freezing hands and enough to buy lunch – although not the whole family's Christmas presents which had been the goal…

Maybe I'm getting old, doing one of those 'its not how it used to be' moments, but hey, move with the times kiddo I say to myself, these guys are living their music and sharing the love and our ears are privileged to hear them.

Are you bemoaning the day today of how 'it used to be and isn't now' or are you going to seize the day with whatever strength you have and say 'well at least I am here so Monday can matter'.

FEEDBACK

Last week Warren made me think… Feedback… we say it's so important and something we say we all embrace, but do we? Really? Honesty in reporting is a manager or leaders' responsibility, but we all know people who have 'hedged' or 'omitted' issues because they feel they don't want to be responsible for someone else's lack of career progression- rather than telling them and helping them to succeed where they might be happiest and most fulfilled doing their best work. Or maybe, we worry we are wrong in assumption in the judgement of another. Or maybe, we don't care, we just want them gone from our environment and someone else can sort out the 'problem child'.

Clearly the opposite is true too, the accolades and abundant superlatives of brilliance and high potential are also hollow in their own way. You care because the person makes you look good, but do you care enough to say 'it's not me, I just guided them, it's their innate or learnt talent that is shining and should be recognised'. How generous are we? Where do our own vulnerabilities stop us being able to be genuinely giving of respect and recognition. Isn't it the duty of every leader to surround themselves with trusted challengers not 'yes' people.

But are you brave enough to do that? To recognise talent you do not have but admire, not envy. Can you acknowledge others today who have put you – and keep you – in the privileged position you enjoy? Or are you stressed to pieces by hanging on by your fingertips to some kind of acknowledgment?

Give feedback where you know you can and should – even when it is hard, especially then in fact. How about starting today. Make Monday matter.

LIVING LIFE

Hello Monday!

I met a man at the weekend who is 81 (and thinks he's 18) and his new wife (nearly a year now) aged 79… The got married last summer, are moving house – no not downsizing to something sensible and 'old people like', but to something that they want to make 'theirs'. He wants to build a sunroom onto one end, convert one of the rooms into a study for him and sewing room for her…There is a big (for anyone with a normal sized) garden, and even outhouses with possibilities for conversion to a B&B! Healthwise, no, they are not doing great either. One has a breathing problem, the other a heart condition, and you might on the face it think this is complete madness! You might be right! But the joy and interest life that they both have, the belief that they are just as young as ever was, the shrugging off of being old is something that is most definitely keeping them moving forward, knowing that they plan for tomorrow and live each day as if it's their last. Learn from the past?! You must be joking! They are only interested in now and the future! And who are we to stop such enthusiasm, joie de vivre and vivacity! Of course, there is always much to learn from the past (my mantra being the past is for reference not residence) but if you want to let it go, move on, then who of us is qualified to stop anyone doing that?! Let us all hope and pray that this Monday matters for this couple, and every other one of us out there who have another week to make a difference and live our lives fully. How will you make your Monday matter?

If you want to read more about this sort of approach to life, I found Atul Gwande's 'Being Mortal' an inspirational read. Chocolate ice-cream and football anybody?... You'll know what I mean when you read it.

BRAVER, STRONGER, SMARTER

My online Pilates teacher has a sign on her wall behind her that says 'Always Remember, you are BRAVER than you believe, STRONGER than you seem and SMARTER than you think' and I love it! Partly because it is that constant affirmation as I look at the screen and stretch into unbelievable shapes, positions and the intervals, repetitions and fear of falling over, falling apart or simply stopping any moment, her 'wall' always centres me back to what I am supposed to be doing… just by looking at it! And the hilarious thing is, the quote is from Winnie-the-Pooh! Which I am told from Google is a 'Disney cartoon fiction'… now just hang on there I thought, I think it's from the children's book by AA Milne isn't it? Well, horses for courses and however different generations access this fabulous saying it really does strike a chord.

Ironically, sometimes other people think I am braver than I am, stronger than I feel and expect me to be smarter than I am… And that's it isn't it… these motifs or prompts are to remind us that actually we are brilliant just as we are!

Sometimes we also think others are braver than they should be or could be, not as strong as they make out or could be and a lot less smart too, but who are we to judge people in that way? We are vulnerable and brilliant, all of us and all of use, the fragility of the human who can achieve amazing things for ourselves (not just in Pilates!) for our loved ones and for those we don't even know but are impacted by how we behave, what we believe and our contribution in the professional and personal space. So let's make this Monday matter together by remembering that you ARE braver than you believe, stronger than you seem and smarter than you think – and so are others!

ROUTINE V BIG MOMENTS

My friend called me on Sunday to talk through her concerns for the result of a breast biopsy and what it might show. Of course, she was anxious about the results and the impact this might have on her, her husband, children, parents, job, and LIFE. But one of things she majored on was the apparent detachment and 'head rather than heart' approach from the clinical teams. Maybe they were or maybe they weren't, but the key is how she experienced the interaction which helped – or didn't – her concerns and big moment about her whole person.

In the NHS there has been much focus on something called 'compassionate care' (and my friend is abroad anyway), but this goes further than healthcare, this matter is relevant to all of us whatever our business. What is it that you do that is routine, that you do many times a day, week or month, but which might be a 'big moment' for another person or business? And how do you make sure it is personal, authentic and meaningful each time.

If we're honest, we don't do it 100% do we? Well, maybe if we are kinder to ourselves, we can say 'we often do', or even, 'we mean to'. How others experience us in a 'big moment' is massively impactful, whether it's positive or negative. The great Maya Angelou said, 'people will forget what you said, people will forget what you did, but people will never forget how you made them feel' and that's surely got to be something to really embed in the way we share what is our routine with another's big moment. Facts and clarity are fine – and necessary – but just because you have had the conversation or done the act over and over, and it seems like 'no big deal' just pause for a moment and ask yourself if that's true for the other end of your action or conversation. This Monday is going to matter hugely to someone because of you, so as Angelou also said "Do the best you can until you know better. When you know better, do better." And now YOU know, so make Monday matter.

– 8 –

LISTENING

Do you have a noise in your head, a sort of itch that needs scratching or a low buzzing that won't go away, a niggly thought and like someone is chain-sawing but far away, yet you can still hear it? Or a bee in a room somewhere that you can't quite pin-point, but you know it's there.

I find it so distracting, to hear the external world buzzing and getting into my head when I am trying to focus entirely on one moment, to be 'present' in order to listen to what is actually being said to me or a thought I am trying to have! Turning the volume down on the extraneous 'noise' and interference – like an old-fashioned crackly radio broadcast and turning up the volume of the actual present moment is a work of a lifetime but one I am committed to and making some progress I am pleased to report.

I do find it really hard to take the yogic approach of noticing the thought and letting it pass. 'What if I forget it?' I worry, 'It might be important to remember it and need to hold onto it'… I find the buzzy bee's do distract and the thoughts of what I must do, might do, didn't do, did do! All come in and try and knock me off course.

So I have turned to a really basic form of learning to listen, and to listen even harder! It really is a the most basic thing we can do with each other. It is what parents do – from interpreting an infant's nighttime cries to reading the subtext of a teen's angry outburst, it is something we can do without words but with intention, you see blackbirds listening for worms in the ground for sustenance and rabbits with their radar like ears listening to keep them safe, all this overriding their need to transmit, as we so often are doing!

So listen, then listen again to what is here, now being said to you, or not being said to you, to the cues of what we call 'non-verbal' communication. Do we really always use our ears and our mouth in the proportion we were given them? Do we listen with our heart as well as our brain? And when we do stop, and actually listen – be it work or even lying on the ground in a park, we hear a deeper level of communication, like seeing more stars in the sky the more accustomed our eyes become to the dark… It is the same. Maybe try to focus on the proportion of listening to transmission this Monday and see what really matters.

ARMOUR

Do you wear armour to work? You know, sharp suit, good haircut, polished nails and neat lipstick? Something that gives that 'Bam'! I am here impact', or 'ssshhhh… I'll just be over here and be invisible' cloak?

What does it mean? What does it give you? Perhaps confidence in yourself, or you think it gives others confidence in you. Perhaps it is to fit in? Or stand out? What is its protection, and does it show only one part of who you are and not make you vulnerable to all the slings and arrows that might come your way?

The Christians have a whole part of their teaching on the 'Armour of God' that it will help the faithful stand their ground when evil things happen. He will give them a belt of truth, a breastplate of righteousness, boots of peace, the shield of faith, the helmet of salvation and the sword of the spirit. And its strangely relevant – we talk about walking a mile in another person's shoes to truly understand them – that's a peaceable act, and the rest of it sounds pretty strong and shouty to be in all that kit. So, although we don't have all the cumbersome metal stuff when we show up to work, we do have the faith that with our armour on, somehow, we are protected.

The Christians believe with their armour on they have the faith that the rest will come, whatever happens, they have God's protection.

Interesting. You can see the armour, and probably hear it clanking along, but you can't see what they believe is the power it gives. A superpower maybe. Maybe your armour is one that others cannot see either, but it might be just as strong. Maybe just knowing Monday matters and you have a clear purpose is enough to keep you, the real inside you – protected and safe.

JACKET

I wore a jacket last week that a lot of people commented on… The colour, style, uniqueness, and some for whom they said 'I have no words I just love it' and couldn't stop looking at it… It's funny isn't it, how something different or unusual can evoke a response… and not just a response, but out loud from a few people who I have never spoken to before, and some I didn't even know…

What propels people to say things out loud? To a stranger?! To feel the urge and need to say a positive thing? To make a personal remark and a complement when usually silence and containment is the default position. I love that. The passion that has bubbled up inside that then spilled out into words of this emotion, to a complete stranger…. Doesn't that bring joy? It makes my heart sing that a piece of creative genius, thought up and fashioned by someone – let's not forget the creator of this garment for I am but the clothes hanger! – has come together, and it brings me immense joy and strength when I wear it, and to others for them to speak out when they see it! The power of creation is extraordinary. And the REALLY secret part about this marvel, is that within that jacket, that no one can see or know except the wearer (unless they are told) is that on the inside, in the centre of the lining at the back there is a printed patch sewn in which states 'The future depends on many things but mainly upon YOU'.

So if you have passion or creativity you feel is dormant inside you, or perhaps you know it's there and screaming to get out but you are still able to contain it, perhaps it is time to let it spill out? Maybe let that urge to say something positive outloud, whatever the stimulus that propels you. Make this Monday matters – to you, or to someone else – because either way it is YOU who are the key to it.

– 11 –

EASTER

Monday matters… or does it??…

Last week my husband said 'will Monday matter on Easter Monday'?,… interesting… Yet again we have a Bank Holiday based around a Christian festival, and yet we are in the middle of Ramadan, and have just seen the appointment of a Muslim as First Minister of Scotland. What has that to do with Easter? (and some of you know I am very keen that people can take bank holidays when it matters to them – Christmas simply 'isn't' for some… My Jewish friend once explained to me that in her calendar there was Simchat Torah and then Hannukah. 'And then Christmas' I said. 'Yes.' she said 'Well, no, obviously not, but yes, for you it is'.…

Historically, Islamic countries have weekends on Thursday /Friday, and have moved it (to help with business, trade and so on) to Friday and Saturday, as in Saudi Arabia and the UAE. So does Monday matter?… Hmmm… yes, it does to me, yes I am a Christian, and yes to many of us who work 'Monday to Friday' '9 to 5' (anyone else hear a Dolly Parton song coming on??) but it has made me stop and think… What matters to me, and matters to some of you simply doesn't even feature never mind matter to others. And why should it? Why should we impose our ways of life or constructs on others? Of course there is something about order and consistency and so on, but I am seeking more and more to dwell a pause and check in with myself more widely around my assumptions to say to myself 'ok, so this is my view, but what might I learn or know if listened to others or sought to live through different cultural norms'? Does Monday matter?… You can decide today!

TRUTH

I have a problem with the truth. The trouble is I really really like it. I really, REALLY struggle when others have what I call a 'loose relationship' with it, and I am not sure just where I sit on the continuum of delusion, economy of truth by omission and then the other end is downright lies. Hmmmmm… actually, I think I do know where I am at that end!

So, at work, should we always tell the truth? Always?

Should you tell the lady on the bus or coffee queue her label is sticking out of her dress collar?

What about the report you haven't quite finished writing - ok, be really honest, haven't started writing – yet? Do you say, 'it's coming along', or 'I'm having some difficulty with it but it's getting there', or do you even 'reclassify' something that sounded like it should have been written to more of an informal, verbal, 'not even in existence' type piece of work?

Clearly, we have governance and 'rules' around telling the truth at work, in accounts, or declarations of interest, and even in being honest with your colleagues in appropriateness of behaviour and inclusion.

But there are also grey areas of advice, thoughts, what I 'might have said but didn't challenge as I just wanted to let it pass even though I knew it wasn't true'? Or the unknown unknowns which might later turn out to be known knowns and with hindsight we chose totally the wrong path...

What is it that tells us when others are doing it to us? How do you feel it, sense it, notice it? Or most worst (if that's a phase!) when we do it to ourselves...! 'He/She/They won't mind really' or 'It's for their own good' (really??) or even 'I don't care what they think' (again, really??).

So in all your interactions today how many times are you going to be utterly completely and wholly honest, and how much will you be fudging it? (Or worse!). Even to the person from the charity on the pavement who wants you to stop and you avoid their gaze or say 'So sorry I'm in a hurry' when you know full well you're not. How about 'sorry, I am not taking on any more charities at the moment' isn't that more honest? Not offensive, just straight forward.

The Buddist frame that I find helps here offers; 'Before you speak, let your words pass through three gates by considering, Is it true? Is it necessary? Is it kind?'... Maybe try it, if you think this Monday matters.

3 WORDS

I was introduced to the app 'What three words' about 3 years ago, the one which has seemingly divided the world (or maybe just UK?) into 1 metre squares and is super brilliant- if not a little odd to start with – to find the exact spot where someone or something is.

So, I was using it to navigate to a new place the other day and I was listening to the car radio and hearing about a friendship going back 50 years, which was also using an exercise to aid memory. It made me smile gently as the carer tested the cared-for on the 3 words she was supposed to have remembered during their conversation, as she was experiencing a progressive dementia. I felt a spring of joy at listening to part in their conversation, so much so that although they were doing this 'remembering' to mine this cared-for person's work for future legacy, I too will now also remember them as a person, even though we have never met, because of the 3 words (painting, candle and table).

And then joy of joys the next sharing was 3 completely NEW words for me 'neuroexpansive, Neuroqueer Theory and Neuromances. Awesome! I turned the radio up. Do you know these words? Is it my white abled-bodied ciss gender hetro-sexual privilege that blinds me or simply hasn't exposed me to them before? Well, I do now! This depth of knowledge, experience, literary genre and a deeper level of life is growing me, I can feel it! I am becoming more than I was before. And isn't that a hugely important and necessary part of knowledge to be an effective ally, to understand the vitality of all!

What 3 words will you hear or choose today? They might take you on a journey of discovery perhaps. Maybe they are the words 'I love you' maybe you should say them? Or maybe it's acknowledging the 'past', 'present' and 'future'? Or maybe change someone's professional life through the words 'Join Our Team'? Whatever your words are, Make Monday Matter.

– 14 –

EXPECTATIONS

I love it when people surprise me! I don't mean a like a party or jumping out Cato style (y'know from The Pink Panther!) I mean exceed my expectations (and of course how awful the feeling is when they don't!).

I had a flat In Manchester from a long time ago, and sorry to say the letting agent has been rubbish. Not paying the rent on, not paying contractors when work needed doing and forever needing chasing on any small task. I don't think he was crooked, just so disorganised and bad at managing money that his cash flow was all over the place, and everyone felt constantly let down and frustrated. So, I decided to get rid of the 'service' being not-delivered and do it myself. I felt quite anxious contacting the tenants who I had heard from the letting agent were 'difficult' but in fact, they were delighted to hear from me as they hadn't been allowed to contact me by the letting agent, and who were forthcoming with their desire to live in the flat, keep a good house, not take the proverbial and of course when they paid rent expected it to get to me!

Now I know there is a perfectly clear neuroscientific explanation for this where our 'error' rate of expectation and reality is positive and the chemicals released brings us the sensation of pleasure – as per the PEPE model of change. What I am referring to is noticing the feeling, that of relief, the gentle involuntary smile and how suddenly everything looks better and brighter and more affirming of our trust in humanity, and so becoming more generous to the next person or task. I wonder if today we might notice our pleasure a little more, perhaps even forgive the ineptitude of others who don't make the grade (once we have dealt with them!), so that the next interaction also benefits from positivity. If you have the gift of feeling positive, why not pay it forward and give that to others to help their Monday matter too.

FROGS

Do you celebrate Frogs? No, not the ones that croak in the pond but celebrate each other 'For Recognising Others Greatness'! How brilliant is that? Calling out someone who noticed someone! I always thought the phrase was to 'eat a frog first thing' meaning that when you get to work in the morning do that think you really didn't want to do first, and then its out of the way and won't be hanging around all day with you dreading to do it! And still having to! But this is a new one on me!

A Chief Executive friend says she likes to 'celebrate frogs' at least once a month! And I am not sure whether the term goes as far as 'being frogged' but it feels like it might! And then I saw it for real the other week.

I was out catching up with an ex-colleague and at the next table to us were two women having supper. My friend and I realised after a few minutes that we knew one of the women! And this person was taking her own colleague out for a meal to thank her for all her work as she was leaving the team. Just her, taking her colleague out, and saying thank you. Surely that is goodness in and of itself. Of course, it is. But then to have my friend (her bosses boss) come in and notice her kindness, recognition and 'good leaving' for this colleague, now

THAT's something to be celebrated – a FROG… And the great thing of course is that as in all these things, everybody learnt a little bit more, felt a bit more positive and affirmed I say that mattered for a Monday.

HOLIDAY

This Monday Matters – all 5 senses are put on notice that they will be used to the full for non-work purposes this week!

I will see the beautiful Highlands of Scotland.

I will hear and smell the sounds and chuffs of steam from the fire celebrating the age of steam whilst enjoying a journey on The Jacobite.

I will be tasting the 'water of life'.

And my heart will be touched for it is my husband's birthday, our wedding anniversary and I am on holiday!

This Monday DEFINTELY Matters!

What senses will you use this week and why???…

HOMELESS

Something amazing happened on Friday night that hasn't left me…

I was walking from London Victoria underground into the station to go home, and I passed a man sitting, head in hands, on the stairs, staring at the floor, asking for money for a hostel… I know, we see a lot of this in London, in a thin tracksuit, poor trainers, no socks, and so often just walked past.

Usually, I have something in my bag like a piece of fruit, or a small packet of biscuits and often offer those, but I don't offer money… I am never sure why not, but mainly I think this is because I worry it won't be spent on things that will help… interesting, who am I to judge what helps another???… and yet, as I walked past, crossed the concourse I realised that maybe, maybe, this wasn't about the money, maybe it was about being noticed and not ignored… The crushing pain of not being seen and hundreds and thousands of people walking on by. Ok, maybe that's naïve and it totally was about the money… But again, why should I only try to help my way? Or give in a way that plays to my narrative rather than in the way that is being asked for…?

So I wasn't sure what to do, 'how can I help?' I thought, so I thought I would sit on the step next to him and ask if he would like company. It's all I had I thought. He could always say no! I went back, touched his arm as he was crumpled on the ground, eyes closed looking exhausted and asked him. I wanted him to know he was a person with value, just by being. "I just want a shower, and to be safe, in a bed, I do know a hostel. I do. Its £16." he said. We talked a little about other places which will provide support and how he had ended up there, from Doncaster, and I decided to do something I never do, I realised that I had £10 in my bag – for emergencies! Ironic, eh? He had £5 in his cup and a man gave him £2 as we were talking. I said, "If you get the money tonight, what will you do tomorrow?" "I don't know" he said, "I am so tired I don't know, but I want to get myself straight". And I believed him. "OK, I'll give you the money" I said, and as I said that a £20 note dropped into his cup. Just like that, from a lady with a black jacket and bobble hat walking by. I couldn't believe it! I felt I had conjured an angel out of nowhere! Both he and I were truly taken aback. I gave him my £10 too (it would have been bad not to). And he said, "God bless you, and her, that's amazing, I can go now" and he got up looking truly SO relieved.

Will he go to the hostel? Will he rest and get his life back together? I have no idea, but I do know that it is amazing what small and apparently insignificant acts can do…. For him, for me, and from her.

So this Monday REALLY matters... From right now, look out for those who need you to do what you do, whatever that is, time, money, a listening ear, an idea, a challenge, anything. Whatever is it that you have the instinct to do, do it, because every moment of ever day really matters, starting right now. Monday matters.

EARPODS

If you have your AirPods / headphones in, why do you think people can't hear you?? I have been listening to months of other people's music, conversations about childcare, divorce settlements – or lack of them! – and quite sensitive commercial conversations. Honestly, it is remarkable how not at all private conversations are.... Do you have HR conversations on a train or negotiate the cost and margin on a piece of work? Do you imagine that because other people have their earphones on they can't hear you? They can! Truly. And it's not ok.

I was sitting in a café on the Isle of Wight minding my own business when a guy starts on a call with his lawyer discussing the elements in his divorce case, the benefits or not of keeping certain information 'in my back pocket for later' and indeed whether the daughter who had told him something in confidence about boarding school should be raised now and then breach trust of her and him even though he wanted to nail the issue with his soon to be ex-wife. Further, I am fully apprised of the shared custody clauses and whether or not there should be an agreement about introducing new partners to the daughter in certain timeframes or not, and how to 'get around' and 'reduce the burden' of maintenance.

Now I know life is busy and sometimes all we have is a quiet corner of a café to have a really time critical call and to sort out decisions we would much rather have in a private space, but really, couldn't we just do that? Choose to have those conversations where others don't need to be a part of – only one part in this case – of the conversation? I have to say it made me sad, for all that pain for that family, it made me cross because my moment of trying to concentrate on crafting a business letter (firing a letting agent if you must know, but actually nobody did know unless they are reading this!) was getting interrupted by 'Sian and Sam's' divorce!!

So if you have your 'ears in' at the moment, can you just take a moment to ask yourself 'whose space or quiet or moment am I interrupting by my calls, music, inability to notice others needs?' Maybe their Monday matters just as much as yours?

IDENTITY

Identity. It's a funny thing… who we are, who we see when we look in the mirror, who we have been or want to be, how others see us – through their own eyes and experience, through their identity. Do we notice? Does it matter? Is who we are at work or at home coherent and aligned? What makes that so, or not?

At the King's Coronation, there went the transformation of man, through Prince, to King, and all so publicly – except for the one intimate moment of one man with his God, and the rest we bore witness to, and accept him as our King (unless you don't, but that's a whole other conversation).

Yet in our own transformations, we seem to do it so gradually, with the occasional leap and bound, but never in the full glare of the public eye, where our work and life is accompanied by millions of people across the world, ALL of the time.

So when King Charles looks in the mirror this Monday after such an extraordinary weekend, where he shared his identity and commitment to be one of service not to be served, I wonder to myself what he will see? Will it feel different? Will he look in the mirror and know that this Monday matters in terms of his first week as crowned King, and that he has no 9-5, Monday to Friday! His 'work' identity will endure, he will take his whole self to work as he IS his work.

How does that translate for us then? Do we look in the mirror and say 'I see who I am, and I am going to change it' Tim Scott the only black Republican Senator would say so. I am truly fascinated that we all talk so often about striving to bring our whole self to work, and yet if the man and now King IS his work, then aren't we too?

The words from the Coronation 'service is love in action' have resonated with me deeply, and as I look in the mirror today I see I have the experience, opportunity and strength to be consistent and clear, create opportunities for service and take to heart Scotts' response to the State of the Union address, where he said "There is no ceiling in life, I can go as high as my character by education and my perseverance will take me."

So what do you see when you look in the mirror? Whatever brought you to right now, take a moment, look at YOU. What does 'being you' tell you about what happens next…? Make this Monday matter.

SIZZLE

"You have to sell the sizzle to sell the steak!!" What a fantastic phrase! I heard it from a 'leading brand' – no not of steak! – But wow how true it is that for us to 'sell' our products, whatever they are, shoes, coffee, professional services, banking, lawyers, health professionals, any leader.

I felt like I had just trampolined out of bed when I heard this energetic pizzazzy juicy full-on phrase (with apologies to vegetarians)! It's the belief, the aura, the smell and zing of the thing not just the 'thing' that creates the sale. And I thought I didn't like sales!

And I don't, I don't like people overtly selling to me, I know if I want something or if I don't, I can't bear people telling me how my life will improve with their product – no, not true, I am ok with that, but people shouldn't a) 'keep me warm' when I am thinking about the possibility, urgh! Or b) think that by keeping on at me that I will buy it! It has the opposite effect in fact!

It's the rational, logical, non-risk taking, not liking to be ripped off and beguiled part of my brain that says 'Do I need this? Do I want this? What's the opportunity cost? Are they right? How do I know?' etc.

Yet a friend of mine – note to self, must get in touch it's been too long – loves being sold to! She told me! I remember years ago I said to her I had to sell a bunch of raffle tickets and hated selling them, so she said, "oh I love it, practice on me…" So, I did… and she bought a book of them! I felt like I had robbed her, but she was delighted! Extraordinary! (Of course, we'll never know if that was my tactic all along ??) However… if you want your Monday to matter, might it be committing to 'sell the sizzle' that is just what you are looking for?

J D I

C'mon, just do it. You know you have to (even want to?)… Yes, you. Don't put it off, again, until another tomorrow, but let's start the week as we mean to go on, and let's face it, there is probably someone out there hoping that you will do the 'whatever it is' or dreading that you won't, or might not, or maybe you are simply losing your credibility with the subject by not 'grasping the nettle' and doing the ask. Ouch!

Wouldn't it be a nice way to start someone else's week by being clear, delivering on the need (good or bad) and so providing the time over the week to reflect and keep reconnecting on the difficult conversation, or which moves the world forward in some way, for you or another? Whatever excuses you have – and I have them too – not doing something is as much a decision as doing something. The 'not doing' is serving you in some way, giving you a rationale or reason to 'not do' which frankly you (we) are hiding behind. So, my question is 'in what way does the avoidance of this task, action or conversation serve you?'

Maybe you don't want to hurt someone's feelings, tell them something you know they don't want to hear, or are afraid of the fall out, or you don't know what they or you will do next, or most awfully maybe you have so little regard for a fellow professional awaiting you or your delivery that they are at the bottom of your priority list. That's the 'I'm busy' excuse in case you missed it. And do you think they don't know this?! Your behaviour and actions (or rather lack of them) is written in bold in their sky that they (or the task) are just not important to you as everything else you're doing... So why not just do it, or tell them you're not going to, rather than ignoring it. I'm not preaching, I'm simply suggesting. So maybe just do it, do whatever it is you have putting off – to help others or even to help yourself! Monday matters.

— 22 —

JOB FREEDOM

Last Monday my friend left her job, without any prompting or hysterics she just, left. And I asked her, 'What are you doing?' 'What about your mortgage?' 'How will you manage?' But also 'How does it feel to just let go and not have a plan?'

And she said, 'I have never felt more sure or happier with a decision other than getting married, and I had no idea how that was going to be and its brilliant!'. Isn't that lovely? She has complete confidence that she has outgrown the usefulness of employment, and she sees they want different things, so she took charge and just stepped away!

Of course, she's not stupid my friend, she has skills and a network and all the ideas enough to burst as so when I asked her what she was going to do she said, 'What am I NOT going to do is the question!' I love that! To wake up in the morning and say 'Bring it on day! What shall we do together?' Her smile and freedom of spirit, her lack of fear of what the world can offer, not what it takes from us, is truly inspiring and if her employer can't keep up with her then yeah, good for you! Go and find work and a contribution to the world with the people who can!

This Monday is definitely going to matter to her whatever it holds, I'm sure of it! Yours? How will you make your Monday matter?

KNOW MY NAME

One weekend morning I met a friend for 'brunch' and a catch up. We chatted, ordered a fresh juice for me and weird green gloopy smoothie for her.

We chatted and ordered coffee, pancakes with fruits, quark and maple syrup – no, I don't know what it is either, but it looked interesting and tasted like plain yogurt!

On our lazy morning went, chatting about inconsequential stuff, drank more coffee and water and whiled away the time… it was summer, we could…

When it came to pay the bill I tapped my phone on the special machine they bring to your table now and said 'Thank you Sabine, that was lovely.' She stopped, still, looked at me and said suspiciously, almost in a whisper 'how do you know my name?'. I paused, slightly confused. "It's on the top of the receipt" I said, "served by Sabine". Her face broke into a radiant and wide smile "wow" she exclaimed "no one has ever used my name here before!" "What? Never?" I was shocked. She shook her head. I asked her how long she had worked her. "3 years" she said, embarrassed. I was, and am, outraged. She had served people like me for 3 years and no one, not one single person in all that time had ever used her name!!! That is simply inhuman and unacceptable.

Please tell me you know the name of the person who serves you coffee, or regular lunch spot. In fact, don't bother telling me, thank them by name for their service and make their Monday matter more than any that has ever mattered before. We are all humans, one human race, one does one job, one another. None is better than another. Please, this matters everyday not just on Mondays.

— 24 —

LIBRARIES

A friend has asked his parents to 'proofread' his writing of a new process and policy manual for his business. He said "It's great having one parent who was a lawyer and loves the detail and precision, noting the fact I used 'imperative' three times in 500 words and made three spelling mistakes, and the other parent is more focussed on tone and style – and used to be a head teacher, so I have the benefit of both have great strengths and are very well suited in different ways."

That's family support I thought! And also noting the appreciation of experience and skill from those that have gone before, acknowledging their worth and ability to assist and support in his own work, which he wants to be the best it can be. I see the Ying and yang of this partnership as a real unification of strength. An eminent naval historian once said of his marriage to his academic botanist wife, it was "a union of two great libraries" and the pleasure can be gained from both. Ian Hamilton Finlay, the 'concrete poet', set his poems in the garden of sculpture created by his wife, and a whilst this is a particularly refined and classical example of the ying-yang it shows tangible form and skill in the

'Repetition, imitation and tradition, exploring the juxtaposition of apparently opposite ideas.'

Do you have an equal and opposite partner? Work colleague, friend? Who when you are together others get more than the sum of the parts? Isn't that the basis of all teaming? I wonder how we can try that this Monday and make the 'matter' even more impactful than we had even dreamed of as one, just by teaming up?

LIMITS

Limit? What limit?

I am filled with joy and utterly humbled to say that I have seen something that makes me know the only limitation we have is that which we perceive of others or give to ourselves.

I saw I young man in a wheelchair with significant all limb spasticity, what seemed to be unstoppable tremors in his body, unable to speak or communicate to the casual observer and with glasses on which covered his almost closed and unfocusing eyes…

I thought I had seen him before, near the heritage railway that I volunteer on, and recognised his parents, calm, patient, loving, pushing his chair and taking in the exhibition with him, or for him. I couldn't tell.

And then between them they seemed to have agreed that this young man would do what everyone else had been doing, at his instigation – which they could understand from him even if I couldn't – that he too would walk down 5 steep stairs, underneath a huge steam locomotive train, along the workshop pit and up the other side…5 more steep concrete steps, and with the obligatory hard hat on of course. Ok, so his Dad went with him, guiding, supporting, but the gentleness, the care, the love, real love for those two people to know their son had this desire and the ability even though to the stranger it looked impossible. They had done the recce, imperceptibly, and there was no fuss or flapping nor resigned anxiety or worry, just gentle love and support for this young man to achieve his goal and aims to enjoy and experience the trains as much as everyone else had.

What might we help others to achieve if we saw beyond our initial limits for them? And what might we achieve for them or ourselves with patient, unfussy care of our fellow human? No limits, I say. Start today, Monday matters.

26

BLUE CAT

Standing on a train platform I am looking down and typing as I can see what looks like a small blue toy cat looking back at me, only the size of a large pebble… Truly, right now. Between the rails, hundreds of trains must have rattled over this little furry friend and there he sits (He? She? They?…) seemingly quite happy but also kind of lost… And what is this little one's identity?

(I am sitting on the train now)… I often see dropped little friends from buggies and prams, and it always makes me sad… not just for the little one who has lost their friend, but also for the giver of the little friend to know it is lost. How the ripples of one dropped toy can cause so much sadness and impact so many… However…

I tend to pick these toys up (not this one, I'd be arrested on the track! But I will say 'hello' next time I am here!), I give them a wash and a name – and the giraffe I found in a hedge (Gerry the Giraffe, of course!) has ended up as a new friend for a Ukrainian toddler who is now in our community. New friends, lost friends, alter egos, even identities made up through play are in my mind this Monday, and wondering whether we actually take them (actually or virtually) to work with us?? Our behaviours can often be childish, however 'adult-adult' we would like to think we are! Look around, who is the lost toy in your world today? You? Others? Isn't it time to pick them up? Or be 'childish' enough ask someone to pick you up?…

Its ok to be not ok, everyone needs a friend, whatever the professional mask we wear in our work. So old or new, lost or loved – or both! – make this Monday matter.

LOSS

It's been a year since my friend's husband died, too young, and leaving a gap in his loving wife and beautiful girls lives. And what is a year? Less than a minute in the clock of life… 365 painful days including birthdays, anniversaries, annual rituals for no reason like going to the beach on New Years Day…

How does time stopping for one person in their passing away create such waves and cycles of emotional movement yet also be stuck as the ticking hand of the clock sticks and cannot tick on when a part fails, or simply departs. Yet life does go on, one breath at a time from moment to moment, and my friend tries to work, to create 'normal' moments when nothing will ever be that 'normal' again.

And this new life begins for my friend and for her children, one which has a path they cannot see or know yet, but the path is there, and they edge along it because day does follow night. That's what life does, it lives. So, as dawn breaks on another week and all that we hope for and know we will do, remember old Father Time and how much of it you give to work to make Monday matter, and sometimes, perhaps, give time elsewhere which might matter more today.

WEATHER

So how's the weather? We love talking about it! Moaning about it, celebrating it. Too hot, too cold, too much rain, not enough, don't care, do care, want to be in it, out of it, can't even see it as my office doesn't have windows! Errr… What?

Just what kind of weather are we talking about here? The actual rain, shine, snow, wind type weather or the "weather" at work? Do we talk about it as much as the actual weather? Of COURSE we do! We just call it. 'Culture' and 'how we do things round here' and we talk in hushed tones of the coming storms or celebrate the heat waves – but not too hot or we'll burn!

And my Dad has this great saying "the rain it raineth on the just and also on the unjust fella, it raineth more upon the just, because the unjust has the just's umbrella"!!

I think that's not about the weather-weather eh? That's about the weather you click onto in Teams/Zoom/ whatever call or walk into in the office… So if Monday matters, what's the weather like with you and what's the forecast?

LONDON BRIDGE

I walked past a woman sitting on the floor in the tunnels leading from the underground to the overground station in one of the London stations. 'Have a nice evening love' she said, 'You too' I replied as I walked past. About 4 or 5 steps on I stopped. 'Just how exactly' I thought to myself 'is she going to have a nice evening when I am going to go home to my nice warm bed and loving husband, and she is going to be there on the station floor all night?'

So as sometimes happens, I turned around, walk back towards her and said, 'would you like something to eat' and pointed to the M&S Food store right next to us. 'Yes please' she replied. 'Come on then' I said, 'come and choose something and I will pay'. So, in we went.

In retrospect it was both the right and the wrong thing to do. I wanted her to have the dignity of choosing her own meal or sandwich, but I also realise now that the choice was almost completely overwhelming for her to even taken in never mind decide on. But she did, she chose a pasta salad. 'And a drink' I said, and she picked up a Coke. As we went round the store people stood back, not in respect but more a recoil and it made me sad and angry. But I stayed alongside her, she beeped the items through, and I pinged my phone at the machine. And we walked out together.

'Thank you' she said as she sat back on her old, stained sleeping bag on the floor. 'Well, I just hope you're evening will be a bit better now' I said and went on to board my train. It was a Monday, at least I felt I had done something that mattered.

– 30 –

FREEDOM

How lucky we are to have freedom of thought and speech and be able to challenge one another and not be silenced and steam-rollered into only hearing what 'those in power' want us to. Now I know that sometimes we have to zip it and not say something which 'oversteps the line' but really? In the western world we can say whatever we like, wear what we like, love whoever we like and be safe in our beds, mostly.

But is it luck? And is it true for all of us, probably not. Our history of fighting for all to have voice, women's suffrage, choices of democracy – however imperfect – gives us some ability to say we have earned our right, but it is almost impossible to know how it feels and looks if you don't know how it feels. From either end of that telescope.

We go to work, and yet there are people in our world who are simply not allowed to, go to work, that is. Not allowed to be who they are and make their contribution – where if you are a woman you are not being able to choose what to wear or when and where to go, or who to meet, and need chaperoning to meet anyone, or a man who feels love for another man and is not allowed to show it, or unite openly, or a person who doesn't have a 'category' and is a person who is comfortable to be both or neither, or someone with skills whose lifeline of employment has just been blown up or destroyed.

Yet we are all able to show up to work being, who we are and not who others require us to be. I am not saying that it is easy and, of course, there is still so much to do to include all whoever they are just as they are, but spare a thought for those for those who are not allowed to be who they are and want to be, and how as they wake to meet another day (and did they sleep?) the safety, employment, and business we are in must make Monday matter for us and for those who are not so lucky.

(Written in the week when Alexi Navalny had his sentence extended from 9 years to 19 years, and the anniversary of the murder of Mahsa Amini, as well as many other atrocities not shared on the media)

EFFORT AND OUTPUT

I was talking to someone yesterday about effort and output… does it matter how much effort you put in if the get the output you are looking for? If the output is easy, it is still the output right?… But what about all that effort when you don't get the output you want or need, or that others ask of you, or even that you ask of yourself… how does that get recognised?

I was brought up thinking output was all and effort irrelevant, it was the achievement that got the points, and then 40 years down the line when I reminded my Mum of this she said 'I think I was wrong about that'! 'Wrong!?' My whole professional life (even from school days) was about outputs not what we now call 'inputs'. 'You can't change the rules now!' I thought!

Are you the person who rewards others – even yourself – for trying, even if you don't succeed? And where does that get you? Is it enough? For you or for others.

Of course, the really important nuance to all of this is that Mum didn't say output, she said outcome. And that's different. That's about impact. So, are we churning out achievements – outputs – and being rewarded for that? Or are we changing the world by making an impact, the outcome?

Whether you are enjoying the UK Spring Bank Holiday and making no effort at all, letting your brain have a rest in order to achieve even more impactful outputs – the outcome – tomorrow, or if you are putting in the effort and others may not see for days, weeks or beyond, isn't it the impact that matters? Think about it. Monday matters.

– 32 –

HOLIDAY 2

So you need a holiday. But you've just had one. Or haven't had one for years, so how do you know you want or need one. What is a holiday anyway?

What do you see in your mind's eye when someone says 'where would you like to go on holiday?' Where you have been before? To enjoying the familiarity? Or definitely not going where you have been before? Maybe conscious of your carbon footprint? Having a staycation? Wanting to be in the sun, out of the sun, by the sea, in the mountains, give me snow! And doing what? Nothing. Really nothing? Or 'nothing' as in reading, sewing, chatting, wandering, running, snorkelling, fishing, climbing, dining in, dining out, binge movie watching, glamping camping, 5-star-ing, being out of your comfort zone, in your comfort zone, with people, without people, with some people, not 'those' people, 'these' people, kids, no kids, big ones little ones other peoples, and sounds, music, tunes, drunken dancing, Dad-dancing 'keep it in tight', please-don't-make-me-dance dancing, silence.

Just what are you trying to achieve here?

For some reason having time away from work is classified as a benefit of coming to work. And yet it is almost a whole project in itself. And too often you come back in desperate need of another one, a different one, the one that you meant to have and yet had the one everyone could agree on. Maybe work out what the 'thing' is that rejuvenates you, that's all, nothing right or wrong, no one judging, so whatever you did or are planning to do, maybe the holiday is the comfort of knowing you can step away from the routine or your 'normal' and that there is a Monday to come back to that matters?

33

PRODUCTION TEAM

I'm thinking today about the people who support me and help me to make Monday matter. I don't mean friends and family, but people like Julie, Chloe and Sarah… my hairdresser, beautician, and postie. These people are the ones who keep my world turning and who are the 'production team' behind the face you see on Teams / Zoom and the ones who make it possible for me to be me, and to show up and want to share and give what I can to you and those I work with.

It's interesting to me that when we talk about who helps us at work and the growth we achieve we think of standing on the shoulders of giants more than those who help make us show up in a tidy professional and organised way! But they are just as important. Einstein, it is said he stood on the shoulders of Maxwell, and Maxwell, in turn, stood on the shoulders of Faraday and, apparently, it was Faraday who said he sat at the feet of Christ for his inspiration. But isn't it funny (peculiar not ha-ha) that we all talk about the successful and influential in our network – be it the inspiring speakers, the thought leaders, those who have made millions (if that's how you count success) but what about the people behind the people?…

Whenever I see Sarah I wave through my home office window, just as I did with her predecessor Josh, and these are people who make our world turn so that my world turns so that I can help turn yours. They also have some interesting perspectives on the world too... Josh was a great horse- racing pundit and although we didn't speak from one week to the next, when it came to Glorious Goodwood he was the man you got your tips from! Thank you for the win last year Josh! And Julie, she's the one that makes me look presentable and gives me confidence that I am looking 'sharp' for public events – and also introduced me to her accountant many moons ago, so that was a win, and Chloe who knows more about waxing than anyone should also has taught me that having high standards really does matter and after she has had a number of rubbish relationships she has now found her prince and is getting married. I couldn't be more pleased and she is blossoming. Life is really full of people who look after us so that we can show up and make Monday matter in our business world. Who makes your Monday matter?

34

PROBLEM OR SOLUTION

Are you part of the solution or part of the problem? Or sometimes both! When a newly appointed Chief Executive friend of mine said to me, "I'm not staying more than 8 years as otherwise I will become part of the problem" the insight this gave me was far greater than perhaps he had intended.

It told me he didn't think it a 'right', or a pinnacle of all he had achieved and so was going to sit there for evermore, nor that he was always right and so wanted to make sure there was room for growth and others to nurture ambition and he would be able to have the generosity of spirit and experience to help them, not stop them.

It told me he wanted to get things done, ride the tricky times as well as see some positive projects through to maturity. It told me he was committed, not afraid of hard work and delivery, yet tempered with too often seeing the merry-go-round come around that it might make him cynical, and to guard against that.

It told me he wanted to work, he liked to succeed, but that success is not always measured by position, title and hierarchy. It told me he knew he had to look after his soul as well as strive and progress forward as it was not the be all and end all to simply be in that role. It told me he was confident he would last that long; he had the energy to go the distance and more.

It told me he knew what matters on a Monday, to him and others. Do you?

– 35 –

PET NAMES

We all have pet names for things, don't we? Or is it just me?? I love it when I hear someone say "pass me the who-jar / whizzer / red-stuff" or whatever they say. It makes me feel like I heard a secret word and had a little glimpse into their life. It's funny how private these words are and yet how we all use them, even in public – we do right? Whether it is a word for a flower, or a food, a family member or an inanimate object!

In my house, we have a 'scrunch' – I know, all very middle class to have a pepper grinder but none the less – I can't remember the last time I said the word 'pepper'. Even buying a greasy spoon breakfast the other weekend morning (oh yes! It's true) I turned to my husband and asked if he'd picked up any 'packets of scrunch'! The paper sachets we are talking here!!! And when in a restaurant he asked the waitress if they had any scrunch, the returning look of befuzzlement made me laughed so hard I nearly had a cow!*

So how can we let others in? Maybe we enjoy the frisson of having the secret language ourselves, at work, in our teams? We can create a sense of belonging by using acronyms, slang and made-up words it's true, and yet also a sense of exclusion too, which is less good. Every industry, sector, group, country, or body of people has a language that makes communication easy or creates barriers. What is your special language at work? Where will it matter this Monday to make sure no one is left out as they don't know what a 'scrunch' is?

*I am told 'nearly had a cow' is a not a common expression either! Who knew?! I've always used it!! Thanks to my friend Jayne's mum when I was 6!

36

SERVICE

I saw a Guy Richie film yesterday (The Covenant if you must know) and I don't usually like this sort of thing, but I found this 'work' and commitment to another human being truly astonishing, uplifting, restoring my faith in what true commitment really means – and it's based on a true story.

Being in the Armed Forces, or any version of wearing a uniform, is a job, isn't it? And it is work, usually hard work. But it's something else too.

It reminds me of something someone said to me 'I don't understand the National Health Service,' they said, 'you wouldn't run a business like that' "Ah," I said, "but that's the thing, it's not a business it's a service". The concept of service is obvious in one way, those in the public sector do it, those in business make money and service comes second. But that's not true, is it? Customer service is very profitable indeed, and what many businesses reputation and therefore growth are built on.

So, can these two be happy bedfellows? Is it more a question of getting the right balance? When does the human action in service of another human trump all other reasons or definitions of work?

I suppose not often and only on extremis – be that rescuing someone or in an emergency. But what about every day? The commitment we make to each other is not about 'the work'. The belief and trust in our fellow human (or lack of it) is not 'work' and the awareness that the thing we are being asked to do is not always as we would like, or for a great reason, even if we signed up to the original principle and it seemed ok for the majority when we started out… and yet, the human spirit, however exhausted, used up or drained seems to have that capacity to inspire and share with us all a lesson of giving and hope which are never overcome.

Wherever you are and whatever your work, thank you for your service to your fellow human to make this Monday matter.

37

SIGNS

There's a sign on the way into my town "Danger – children" and I am sorry to admit it always makes me smile... they're not that bad, honestly! And worse, the adverts that end 'always keep away from children' Is that general advice or something specific about chemicals? My mum's favourite was in an apartment block where a sign read 'residents refuse to be put in bins' – you bet they do!!! And so much we say can get so misunderstood, taken the wrong way and even cause offence.

I think it's particularly hard for people for whom English is not their first language or a different English – Australians, Americans, Africans, Indians, Canadians, New Zealanders... I never got over the use of the words 'pants' or 'fanny pack' when I was at school, but as I got older it was the funny clever not the funny purile that made me laugh, and then as I have got even older we complete the circle with a London bus, the 211 – which you might think is the two-eleven, or the two hundred and eleven, but every time I see it I think "one one was a racehorse, two two was one two, one one won one race, two two won one two" Its Pavlovian!

So what do you say that makes no sense, or complete sense to you but is utterly ridiculous to your colleagues? Have some fun, it's Monday, it'll be round again in a week and so why not have some fun – even if others don't get it, make it matter just for you!

38

WEDDING DITTY

You know that wedding saying, 'Something old, something new, something borrowed, something blue, and put a sixpence in your shoe'? Well, I wonder if we used it as a leadership or management tool, we might get some 'happily ever after' results?

I am known for saying that the past is for reference not residence, and I think that there is so much to learn from experience – our own and others, and if 70% of our adult learning comes through experience then perhaps there are the 'old' ways of doing things to be recognised, but not be the speed bump to progress.

We need something new all the time, innovation is key to any progress and 'ah ha' moments help us move from candles to light bulbs!

Something blue, now here's the thing – is it blue sky thinking? Imagining yet unthought thoughts or the currently unthinkable? Are you going to challenge yourself to some? Or maybe it is the sea – which we think of as blue, but appreciate that a brown North Sea is dirty or foamy Southern Ocean is often blacker and menacing – but the sea takes us to new horizons and lands afar, leaving old countries or habits behind? We can think fondly of them, or not, and move on.

And putting a sixpence in your shoe? A safe investment I say. No, it wont grow, and no, it won't make you rich unless you do something with it, but then, it will hold its value and be enough to get you out of trouble. Its not flashy cash, its not 'on show' but it gives you a sense of security and contentment to know you have just enough.

The combination of these ingredients is intended to create a happy marriage and a good start, so maybe something that matters this Monday.

— 39 —

SLEEP

I have got to sleep! I don't care what you call it, a shavasana, a siesta, an LLD (Little lie down), I've got to have one... Immediately if not sooner!

That's how I felt after facilitating a whole day Board development day last week... I got home and simply had to sleep... emails piling up, task list stretching out beyond the horizon, people on the radio talking about the 'silly season' where you can't get anything done because the politicians or decision makers are on holiday, and I just had to shut my eyes, shut the world out, and let... go...

Silence.

Peace.

Nothing.

50 minutes later, I woke slowly... noticing the end of the blue sky through the window and fluffy clouds scudding past... The rest of the late afternoon still there, and a quietness in my head...

I had given it all I realised, all day, all 13 of them, had all of me. And I was utterly spent. And then it felt good. Good that I had been so present, committed, engaged and sharing everything I had in the moment, not shrinking from tricky issues that were coming up but noticing, carefully navigating and gently getting through some choppy waters with them to the safety of a new harbour the Board could get to know and continue their journey from.

And today is now a new week, a new day, a new Monday, and as wrung out as I felt after that day, I intend to make this Monday matter just as much and go again to give all I have all over again. You only have today to make this day the best it can be, so make Monday matter if you think it does.

40

SMALL CONTRIBUTIONS

I was cleaning a huge steam locomotive engine last weekend in a static display at the heritage railway I volunteer on – you know, like Flying Scotsman, but for 'them in the know' it was a BR Standard 4 – firstly a dry dust then a mix of oil and paraffin using rags to make it shiny. A mid-aged woman walked past me, a member of the public, seemingly looking around the shed, with a roll of kitchen roll under her arm and a wiping a number of the other engines where she could see, and reach, any dust.

'Thanks' I called down from my engine and smiled at her. 'It's nothing' she said, looking to the floor not meeting my eyes 'silly really but just wanted to help, a little, even though he's gone now. My Dad. Used to be a driver here and we'd come here when I was little.' And she was gone around the back of another engine...

It made me smile 'that's lovely, and really, thanks, help is always appreciated here!' I called out.

I wondered what her story was, the sad but warm tone to her voice and with a hint of happy past memory and the honour she was paying it, just quietly on her own, connecting and feeling safe somewhere she belonged (even though I do feel a bit guilty for gate crashing her moment by interrupting it). So, let's be kind today to someone doing their best or having a go or even for making a tiny contribution to goodness. Don't vilify them for being inadequate or not enough. Maybe they need to belong or have a story that goes much deeper than their action, maybe it's all they can do to manage the pain or keep something alive in themselves. Whatever your view, look out for those making their small contribution today as they are trying make Monday matter, as we all should.

41

RESTAURANT

A friend of mine went to a highly acclaimed restaurant last year. Most unusually it was awful, and he complained. But what is most important is the response he got…. No "you should feel privileged to be in our restaurant" or any other arrogant reply, but a full and abject apology, including refund, and sincere reflection on falling below their exceptional standards.

Due to this fulsome and humble response, my friend booked again this year. On arrival, they remembered him (now that's personal service!) and said how delighted they were that he had chosen to return and that they would ensure he had the food and service that was so lacking last year. And indeed, it was. It was exceptional!

We all make mistakes, misspeak, upset people and get it wrong, and that's ok, we are humans! It's how we deal with it that matters. I find the least secure folk tend to make the most defensive noises and justifications and worry that they will lose face, or won't be trusted any more, or even somehow will be taken advantage of because they've messed up so dare not show a little humanity. Whereas the true leaders and those who will be respected, trusted and supported will be able to say "sorry, for that one, I got it wrong, let me try again" and it is then for the wronged to match that humility with acceptance. Amy Edmundson and others talk about 'failing fast' and learning from it and I agree, but really, as people, it is as simple as whatever mistakes you make today or this week – and you will – set your intention to repair it quickly, honestly and do better next time, as every interaction, deliverable or day – and in particular Monday – matters!

42

THROUGH CHILDREN'S EYES

My nephew was in the back of the car the other day being suspiciously quiet when suddenly he said, 'Do insects fly when they're asleep?' Staring straight ahead at the dual carriageway… 'Mmmmmm' was the only noise I could immediately muster.

Then my husband chimes in 'I'm not sure insects do sleep'… What?! That wasn't exactly helping my 'Crikey, where do I go with this which might be vaguely right and not ruin this poor little mites chances of becoming a world famous insectologist' thoughts!!

'Why do you ask?' was my first attempt – ignoring husband!

'Well, they keep flying into the windscreen don't they and they wouldn't if they were awake would they?'

Husband "Well, what if we are chasing them and catching them up, then they might be awake maybe?"

Nephew, "Yeah, good point".

Me, "Shut up darling. No, not you darling him darling!"

Husband turning round to nephew and pointing at him pulling a silly face "Nah, she means you".

Nephew giggles.

Me, "Hang on! How am I suddenly in the wrong, you're the ones who don't know if insects go to sleep?!".

Both of them fall silent. I am wondering if that is because they think I know about sleeping insects and they're stuck because they don't, or if they think this is as fatuous as I do, so have ceased being ridiculous. Not being sure that I wanted to check I change the subject to a cheery "So who wants pizza when we get in?" Both "YEAH!" Smiles. Quiet.

Nephew 5 miles later, "But even the flowers go to sleep at night, don't they, when they fold their petals up? "True" I concede, my eyes narrowing almost imperceptibly…

Nephew, almost to himself, "I wonder what it would be like to never go to sleep?"

Me, shooting Husband that look says 'if you speak right now then you are going to be doing long LONG sleeping from about immediately' I say "Well, let's see how that goes after your bath and pizza shall we?" As I am feeling on pretty safe ground with that one!

Does this remind you of any meetings you go to? It feels way too familiar to me!

I wonder, could we try and let whoever it is ask their perfectly reasonable question from their perspective today even though from the listener it seems way out there? It truly matters to their Monday even if not a jot to yours.

– 43 –

T C R

Now those of you who know London might know precisely where I mean and had this EXACT feeling, for others, it's more the feeling than the 'London thing' so do join us!

Last night I caught a bus down, yes DOWN TCR (Tottenham Court Road for the uninitiated!) and I felt all sorts of 'out of sorts'! Down the Up??! For that is what it was, well, IS, for me! I was not happy AT ALL!!

There I was, minding my own business, sitting on the 73 bus, looking out of the window into the patient cafe and pharmacy of UCLH as I was coming in from Euston toward Oxford Circus and suddenly, no more one way up Gower Street and the other way down TCR, oh no! The bus turned UP TCR! What?!! I wanted to jump up and down and tell the driver he had made a terrible mistake! It's one way, it's always been one way, you can't go up the down!… What about all the people coming towards us…?!! Except of course, that's not true anymore is it??… The rules have changed! Probably did years ago, and I simply didn't know or didn't notice, and I felt like no one had even asked what I thought.

Over a decade ago I lived just off that very road, in what my friends call 'The Goodge Street years'. They were fun and many – the friends and the years. But those days are past… there has been a change, and to be honest I felt rather very confused, and in truth, a little 'old'… It has been 10 years (ok, more) since then… since 'vino collapso' and other tales to tell, pre the new Tube line and new station… when the Dominion Theatre was playing 'We will Rock You' and I could walk home from Soho in the wee small hours without a thought… So this feeling caught me unawares and off guard.

As it turns out I am actually a fan of the change that has happened, and usually I am the optimist that looks forward to progress and all that is new, but just for a moment I had a wistful longing for a bygone age of irresponsible freedom, the world there for the taking, and a one way system which I knew I knew!

Of course, if you're me, I then start to thinking about the care I, we, need to take when changing parameters with people in our work life, our home life, our life life… and how I need to make sure I remember this moment when imposing or considering change for others, in all that I do… they may not know or be ready. Or they may be ready if I kinda mentioned it before turning 'the wrong way' up their one way street… and so what might I do to not bounce them into change…?

This Monday, as every Monday, there will be changes – wanted or unwanted, it is how we walk with others in the moment they reach that change that matters. Isn't it? Mondays Matter.

Postscript – Although I started this on the bus, straight away, to tell you of my angst, I finished it later, having crossed the diagonal pedestrian crossing right across Oxford Circus that was never there in 'the Goodge Street Years' and thought "this is better, how efficient"... ah... what contradictory beings we are eh?

ENFORCED FUN

I am embarrassed by jousting, kids theatre, musicals and re-enactment. I know there is absolutely nothing wrong with any of them, and each brings joy to thousands (probably millions) of people, but I just can't go there. I keep seeing a sign for the annual jousting event – party? celebration? near me and I am so seized up by it that I can't even look it up and check the nomenclature!!! If I did the blooming search engine will start sending me other 'events' like it and make it worse!!

Do you remember when you were little and your mum or gran would say 'don't step on the lines or the bears will get you'?! (Ok, so maybe just mine!) But it's that kind of scary! I SO wanted to step on the line yet so afraid to, what if the bears did come and eat me up!? What a waste! I have so much to do! I can't get eaten by a bear when I was told not to?!!! Probably a little over sharing there, but the point is there are things I simply can't and won't do (it's ok, I'm over the treading on lines thing!) but one of the frightening things about the musicals at any rate is that I seem to know all the words too! Aaaagghhh! It's a relief there are so many new ones that I am desperately trying not to hear or learn the words to... No I will not 'Let it go'... aaaaggghh! They give me the screaming abdabs! (I love that old fashioned expression and don't even know what it means! Maybe nothing!) But really, really must we always engage with the things that make us shiver and shriek and want to 'run for the hills' (there you are, another one!) perhaps this new world of strength-based development and experience has got something eh?

Let's not keep battling the stuff that sends us into a spin, let those who love the things that we don't, truly enjoy them, fully and without fear or distraction, but please 'enforced fun' (as I see it!) is not for everyone, so maybe if you have an intention in that direction today, make someone else's Monday matter by not insisting they come or will miss out if your 'thing' is not theirs.

− 45 −

FAILURE

Monday Matters.

We all fail. ? Odd start you might think… starting the week talking about failure, but hey, we know what it feels like… And SO much more difficult on a Monday somehow! Is it about you? Or is it about what others have 'done to us' (or we have allowed them to?!) Did we blame others for last week and say 'I failed because 'THEY' didn't help / weren't good enough / didn't listen and so on… Well, all of that may be true, but here we are again, Monday, and why is it that we carry others judgement into the week and feel so down about it?… I say to you, this week, try saying to yourself when things don't go right or an injustice or slight is done to you by others, say of 'them' "I am sad for them that they cannot see me for I want to bring light to those in dark, narrow, unseeing places" and say to yourself, "failure is one step closer to getting it right, one more step of learning".

Those that cannot see and judge you, be sorry for them, for their limited outlook. Those who can see you (Sawubona!) let them see ALL of you, the strong and lithe steps, the faltering and unsure steps, the falls and the pick-me-back-up steps… THIS is what Mondays are for... We start again. Look in the mirror, look back at last week, be present in this, and look forward to next. Tell yourself 'I see you'. Honour who you are, where you came from, what you bring (tiny or ginormous moments) and what you are going to do this week that is learning from the last. Did you fail last week? Maybe. But the strength and triumph is learning this week to build on that.

Try it. Monday matters, so make it matter for you (you don't even need to tell anyone! Its all about you!! ??)

46

STANDING TALLER

Who makes you stand taller? When you think about a role model you have followed or want to emulate, who comes to mind... I find this hard, because no one is 'me' and I am not sure I see more than 10-50% of perceived role models either. I tried to really come up with one the other day, and I wanted to merge Margaret Heffernan with Elon Musk and Maya Angelou, and I not yet entirely sure of the proportions of each!

However, there are people who make me stand taller, whose work I rate and is highly acclaimed, but what I have come to realise is that what makes all great people great – in my humble opinion – is their underpinning values and drive.

You might admire someone for running a successful company, or making money more than you could ever dream of, but if they have done it by stepping on or exploiting others, or not being honest, they're not really that admirable are they?

Or a captain of a team, like the sports stars we see, are they creating heroes in their team or wanting to be that hero – I saw an interesting illustration of that in the 2023 Ashes series. Maybe we like the sports star who hits rock bottom and then returns better (Steve Smith perhaps?) because as humans we love a story where good triumphs over evil.

I often ask myself, what these hugely public beacons of light and success do the morning after great successes? Get up, brush their teeth, decide what's for breakfast… So maybe we could reverse that, and we could all get up, get ready for the day and make some really big moments today, just like these guys did yesterday, because Monday matters.

47

SOUNDTRACKS

'Well at least it's not Monday' said the lady next to me when the train was delayed, and I mean really mucked-about-delayed-no-information-then-no-driver type delayed. So, what's that about? What's so bad about Mondays... I really wondered what she meant... and in my head I heard a song coming on... "Tell me why I don't like Monday's" (Boomtown Rats). It's a dark song, which Geldof said came to him as 'not liking Mondays' was the reason the perpetrator gave for causing the atrocity in Cleveland Elementary School in 1979. But it got me thinking... About music and soundtracks of life and moments, memories, brands and people!

You know how it is, I have a friend (he knows who he is!) who got me into Steps (yes, the band) as my running music! And I now can't go for a run without him! Not actually him coming with me, he's hundreds of miles away! But in my ears!! Three times a week I think of him! Another was an Ultramarathon runner who finished the Badwater Ultramarathon (135 miles across California's Death Valley – clues in the title!) and at the after-run-party they played Black Eyed Peas 'I've got a feeling'. Yet another was from an inspirational coach masterclass 'What have you done today to make you feel proud'. I love these moments when I hear snippets of these songs as they remind me of those times and people.

And yet I get SO discombobulated when I hop in the car and my (otherwise amazingly beautiful and lovely) husbands has left Radio 2 or Classic FM on the radio blasting out! It's not that I don't like either (although Magic 105.4 still seems to be car radio of choice after Radio 4!) it's that I am surprised by something that might not match my mood, how I am feeling…

So I am choosing my soundtrack carefully this week… My default is 'This is me' (from The Greatest Showman) – probably says the most about me! If I am feeling low or just want to smile I might have a blast of Stuart Townend 'In Christ Alone', Anna Kendrick 'When I'm gone' also makes me smile at the possibility of life and always gives me hope. So I am setting a challenge to myself – and you can join me if you like? – to choose how I feel, choose my soundtrack for the week. These moments start with Mondays. Monday Matters!

48

WHERE PEOPLE ARE

True story. A few years ago, a young woman walked into a church, finds the vicar halfway down the rows of seats and says "Is it possible for you to marry my other half and I please? He has been married before and I have not." The vicar sighs and says, "I am so sorry, I am delighted you want to marry and would love to marry you both together in the sight of God as you wish, but in this area, we don't allow people who have been married before to marry in our churches, even if their betrothed is previously unmarried." The young woman and vicar walk back toward the door when the vicar turns to the woman and said "Don't give up on us, we as a church are so far behind the times. I do wish we would meet people where they are, not where we think they should be".

Interesting isn't it, how institutions, made up of people, with compassionate and loving intention can get it so wrong, and the difference between worlds create such a division in something so unifying as marriage. I often think we might be similar in our own professional lives. Wishing things were different, judging others for having the wrong background, or tie or degree or lunch choice?

Look around you. What will you do today to meet someone where they are not where you think they should be. How might that grow you? And how much could or will your action matter to someone else's Monday? Probably more than you will ever know.

49

WHOLE SELF

I used to be a big fan and advocate of bringing your whole self to work… And now I am not so sure. Maybe its just me, but there are parts of me that I think are not either helpful or flattering to my professional 'persona' and there are parts of me that if I was 100% authentically who I am I would be taken advantage of and might end up hurt or sad.

So it's a balance. Sometimes I want to say to someone 'don't be so ridiculous' when they are exposing a fear or, in my humble opinion, a perception which is off the wall and lacks reality, but I am not sure that would be most helpful – either in that moment or in our relationship. Sometimes I want to talk about the things that are bothering me, from little things like the need to mow the lawn, the cat needing a jab, buying some rice on the way home, and frankly I never liked Steve from accounts as his shoes squeak when he walks… No, I don't think you need all that from me do you? You don't need to know how crowded my head is and all the 'chat' going on in there. You want to see a professional focussed person who delivers and meets or exceeds your expectations. You don't want to be thrown off balance by my emotional dramas or excitements. So how much of ourselves should we bring to work? What is just enough to be human and real but not 'over-share'.

A long time ago I was a Samaritan, on the phone lines and we had this brilliant approach of 'leading in' to a shift and 'leading out' after. It meant that as you arrived you called your leader, and checked in, how was your day, anything to share… And then got on with being entirely present and there for the callers, and at the end of the shift, calling the leader again and talking through the calls, what they were, any triggers and anything I wanted to say. Then leaving and leaving the calls behind so they didn't create a difficulty for the volunteer. The amazing thing about this approach is that I still find it quite hard to remember any of those calls I took, although some I know were very distressing, as I had a way of being me, but also creating some compartments to put things in – my life initially, then focusing on my role on the calls, then leaving that and picking up me again as I left… I wonder if we took a little of that type of approach to our work and wider life we might be able to be more productive at work and more present and relaxed in our wider lives… What would Monday look like then? Would we achieve more and make it matter more?

50

WORDS

There are some words and phrases that give me that teeth grinding 'grrrrrrr' reaction every single time I hear them. The most hideous of these is using any word – adverb, adjective or anything else – before the word 'unique'. You cannot be very unique, quite unique, or anything else unique. Either the situation or person is unique or they're not. Full stop!

Same is true of my reaction to overusing words such as 'iconic' and 'unprecedented'. These words are bandied about, particularly in sports commentary I notice, but surely the more hyperbole we use the more diluted it becomes and the less it means what it means – if you see what I mean! Then there is the use of 'like'… Like is a simile or synonym, not a 'filler word'… and finally, when I hear the phrase 'well I would say…' No! Either say it or don't say it – and politicians are particularly bad at this one – in answering a question the answer is not 'Well I would say', and then saying what you are actually saying. What is wrong with 'I think' 'I believe' or 'I have a number of views on this and…'

I have, in my explorations however also learned new words and phrases, some of which I am not sure I agree should be words (?) but phrases such as 'hellscape', 'nearlyweds' and one of which is my new favourite for the year 'ogments' – you know, orange segments... It's a great word!

So how about this whole special day that is before us we try to make Monday matter by using words the way they are meant to be.

51

SOMETIMES YOU CAN

Somehow it happens. Sometimes when you think you can't do something, it turns out you can. Sue Mott (tennis journalist) called the annual LTA Wimbledon tennis championships "a gladiatorial brutal battle dressed up as a vicar's tea party". I get that. The competitors totally out there alone on that tennis court and throughout the journey of the great champions and the almost-champions there is an energy, a gear shift up, an urgency and energy that MUST be found to get through when you haven't got anything left, and there must be more.

In the reflections on 1980s players – and who remembers Bjorn Borg and John McEnroe as players not commentators? – they had such an interesting perception on the world of what they were doing and why, with hindsight of course! They shared being able to hear and not hear the crowd as they needed to, to absorb the cheers and not let the 'boos' in. The training, of Borg being 5 hours a day on the court and McEnroe nowhere near the same yet had his successes too. There are different ways of writing the outcomes of course, history is pretty much always written by the victors, but I think Mirian Marcales has it about right when she says ,"Fame can damage people but also release them, it depends what type of character you have".

I hope with all the passing of those for whom fame has been, and for those for whom it is to come, that the release and growth is one that then enables folks, like you and me and those we lead and know, to reach back and reach a hand to help others up, to mentor and share, to campaign and advocate for others and to make every day matter like Monday does.

– 52 –

WORK AS A RELATIONSHIP

So what work are you doing today? And more importantly, why? I am sure you choose your career, business area or industry out of a passion or interest? And perhaps a little aptitude? So why is it that work is so frustrating and there is so much focus on how hard it is, the psychological contract between employers and employees? Isn't it just like any other relationship?

You are attracted for whatever reason, looks like a good match, or even meets most of your criteria so you 'swipe right' (or is it left?!). You choose them, they choose you, and then you begin the relationship together. Initially everyone is hopeful and a few good dates – perhaps a few dodgy habits to be sorted out (theirs and yours no doubt!) and everyone tries to behave well, get along and deliver whatever the output is that you / the company said you wanted. So, when does the honeymoon period end? Why does it end? Does it have to end? And I suppose, how can you revive a relationship in a bit of bother... before one or other steps out of line and is apparently 'unfaithful' in the eyes of the other.

Then it's 'it's not you it's me – I need more stretch, opportunity, challenge, care and kindness' or perhaps 'it's not me it's you – you want to much and don't give enough back, you think you can treat me like this etc etc!'

So how is your relationship with your work today? Going well? Needs an honest conversation? Perhaps you need to tell the other side of your relationship what matters to you? What will you do today to make your relationship with Monday matter?